20 WAYS TO DRAW
EVERYTHING

WITH **135** NATURE THEMES
FROM CATS AND TIGERS TO TULIPS AND TREES

LISA CONGDON + JULIA KUO + ELOISE RENOUF

A Sketchbook for Artists, Designers, and Doodlers

QUARRY

Quarto is the authority on a wide range of topics.

Quarto educates, entertains and enriches the lives of our readers—enthusiasts and lovers of hands-on living.

www.QuartoKnows.com

First published in the United States of America in 2016 by
Quarry Books, an imprint of
Quarto Publishing Group USA Inc.
100 Cummings Center
Suite 406-L
Beverly, Massachusetts 01915-6101
Telephone: (978) 282-9590
Fax: (978) 283-2742
QuartoKnows.com
Visit our blogs at QuartoKnows.com

10 9 8 7 6 5 4 3 2

ISBN: 9781631592676

This content first appeared in *20 Ways to Draw a Cat* by Julia Kuo, *20 Ways to Draw a Tree* by Eloise Renouf, and *20 Ways to Draw a Tulip* by Lisa Congdon (all Quarto Publishing Group USA Inc., 2013).

Design: Debbie Berne

Printed in China

MIX
Paper from
responsible sources
FSC® C016973

CONTENTS

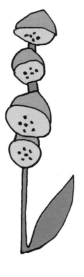

INTRODUCTION

Let's learn how to draw EVERYTHING together! There are few things more fascinating and beautiful on earth than animals, flowers, plants, and trees. They come in all shapes and forms—from tiny birds to gigantic elephants, elegant tulips to wild orchids, geometric snowflakes to patterned pinecones.

Like most things in nature, these subjects have both organic and geometric qualities, as well as naturally balanced compositions. Learning techniques to render them can be a really enjoyable, inspiring experience.

This book is divided into three sections with 45 themes in each, though you will see that there is some overlap. Each of those themes features 20 examples of ways you might draw it. All in all, there are 2,700 images in this book to inspire you!

Even something as simple as a leaf comes in so many varieties that it's impossible to draw just one kind. At first glance, a collection of maple leaves might look very similar, but if you look closely, you will notice that each one has individual features, different angles, and unique veins.

HOW TO USE THIS BOOK

No matter what you decide to draw first, you will soon realize that each item presented is made up of a combination of lines, shapes, and patterns. To begin, look for squares, circles, straight lines, and squiggly lines to help break down the pictures, then try copying different drawings using those simple elements.

Draw the big shapes and lines first, then add in the smaller details. If you have tracing paper, you can trace the drawings directly—and don't worry about getting them exactly the same. Then, when you think you have gotten the hang of it, try drawing your own!

When examining a drawing of a flower, you might ask yourself: How many lines and circles do I see? You might break down the elements: What shape are the petals? Is the flower symmetrical? How can I render the interior stamen? Do I want the stem to appear straight or crooked? Are the leaves perfectly uniform or slightly askew? There are so many quirks in nature, and including those quirks will make your drawings much more interesting!

Start out with a pencil and eraser so that you're not afraid of making mistakes. When you feel more comfortable with drawing, explore different types of tools—pens, colored pencils, markers, paints. Color in the existing drawings and then your own. If you are feeling especially adventurous, you can cut out paper shapes and paste them on the blank pages. It's always fun to try as many things as possible to decide what you like the best.

See how many different pictures you can come up with of your favorite plants and animals. How many ways can you draw a turtle shell? You can make it a circle, square, or irregular shape. Think about what you can draw inside the shell. You can fill it with stripes, little spots, big spots, squares of different sizes, or just a solid color. You can also decide to draw nothing inside the shell if you think it looks best that way!

Don't forget to show your friends and family when you're done. Or even better, ask them if they want to draw their favorite EVERYTHINGS too!

SECTION 1
ANIMALS
Illustrations by Julia Kuo

DRAW 20
cats

DRAW 20
TROPICAL BIRDS

DRAW 20
Giraffes

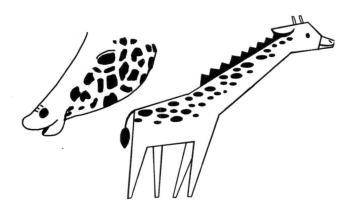

DRAW 20

elephants

DRAW 20
Songbirds

DRAW 20
BUGS

DRAW 20
BEARS

DRAW 20

DRAW 20
DEER

DRAW 20
octopi

DRAW 20
DOGS

DRAW 20
rabbits

sheep

DRAW 20
SQUIRRELS

DRAW 20
LIONS

DRAW 20
TURTLES

DRAW 20
tigers

DRAW 20
RHINOCEROSES

DRAW 20
frogs

DRAW 20
Raccoons

DRAW 20
FOXeS

DRAW 20
hedgehogs

DRAW 20
jellyfish

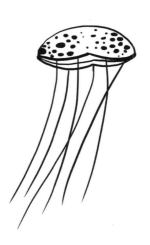

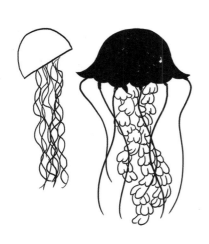

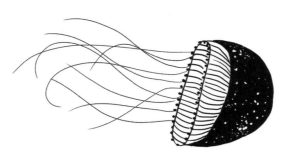

DRAW 20
Kangaroos

DRAW 20 *Lizards*

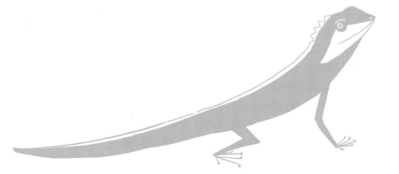

DRAW 20
ZEBRAS

DRAW 20
llamas & alpacas

DRAW 20

BUFFALOES

DRAW 20
mice

monkeys & apes

DRAW 20
OTTERS

DRAW 20
Birds of Prey

DRAW 20
OSTRICHES

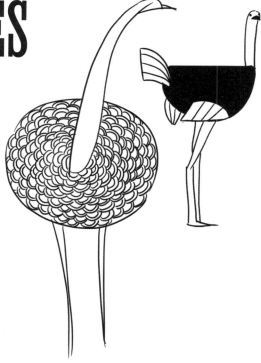

DRAW 20
Skunks

DRAW 20
WHALES

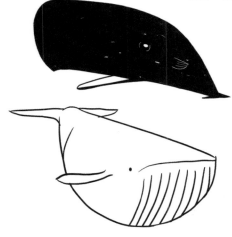

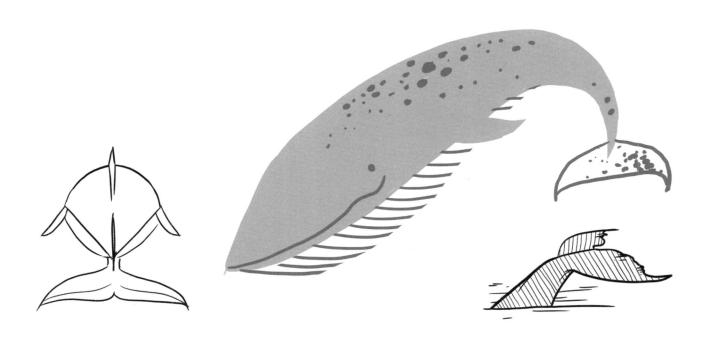

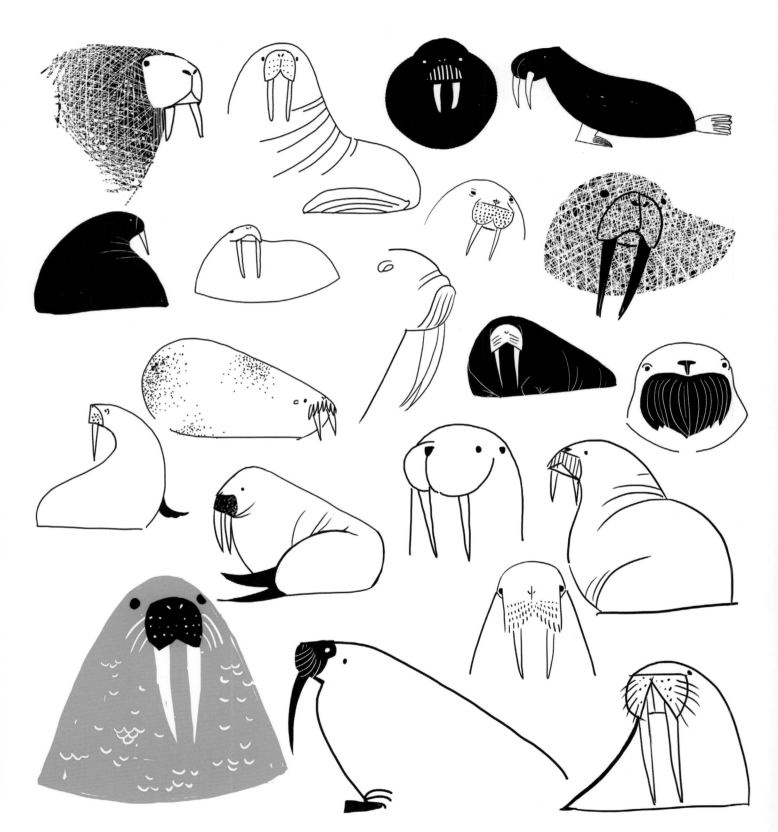

DRAW 20
walruses

DRAW 20
HORSES

DRAW 20
hippopotamuses

DRAW 20
FLAMINGOS

DRAW 20
PIGS

DRAW 20
penguins & puffins

SHARKS

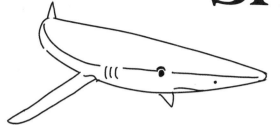

DRAW 20
camels

DRAW 20
sea lions

DRAW 20
snails

SECTION 2

NATURE

Illustrations by Eloise Renouf

DRAW 20
TREES

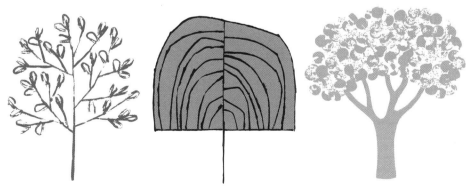

DRAW 20
mushrooms

DRAW 20
Birds

DRAW 20
stemmed flowers

DRAW 20
Ferns

DRAW 20
PINECONES

DRAW 20
LEAVES

DRAW 20
acorns

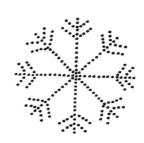

DRAW 20
SNOWFLAKES

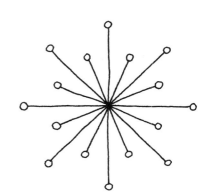

DRAW 20
berries

DRAW 20
Herbs

DRAW 20
snails

DRAW 20
FEATHERS

DRAW 20
Winter Trees

DRAW 20
daisies

DRAW 20
Owls

DRAW 20
Beetles

DRAW 20
flowers

DRAW 20
CLOUDS

DRAW 20
apples

DRAW 20
GRASSES

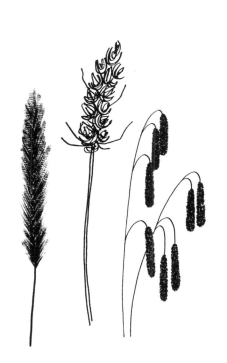

DRAW 20
tree seeds

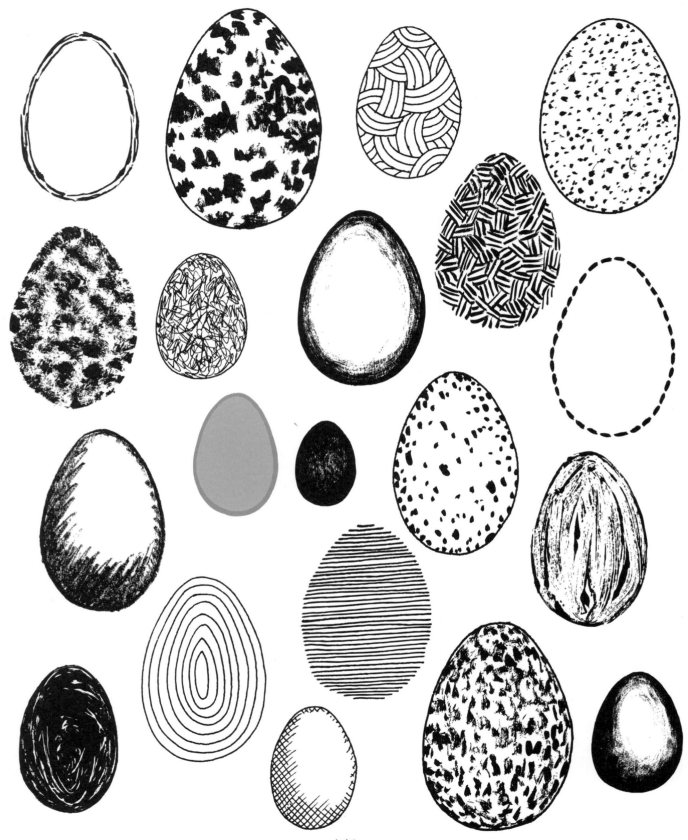

DRAW 20
eggs

DRAW 20
shells

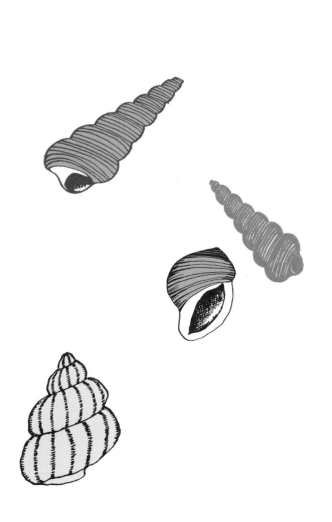

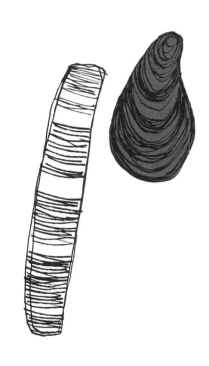

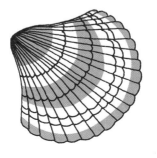

DRAW 20

logs

DRAW 20
STARS

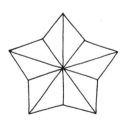

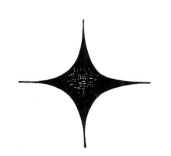

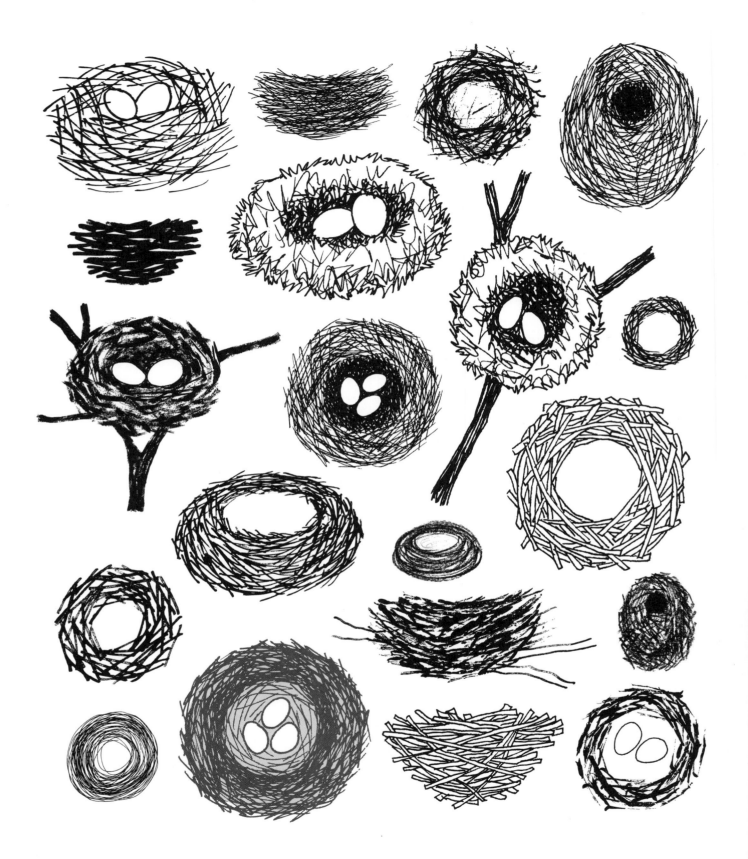

DRAW 20
nests

DRAW 20
roses

DRAW 20
FOSSILS

DRAW 20

blossoms

DRAW 20
STONES

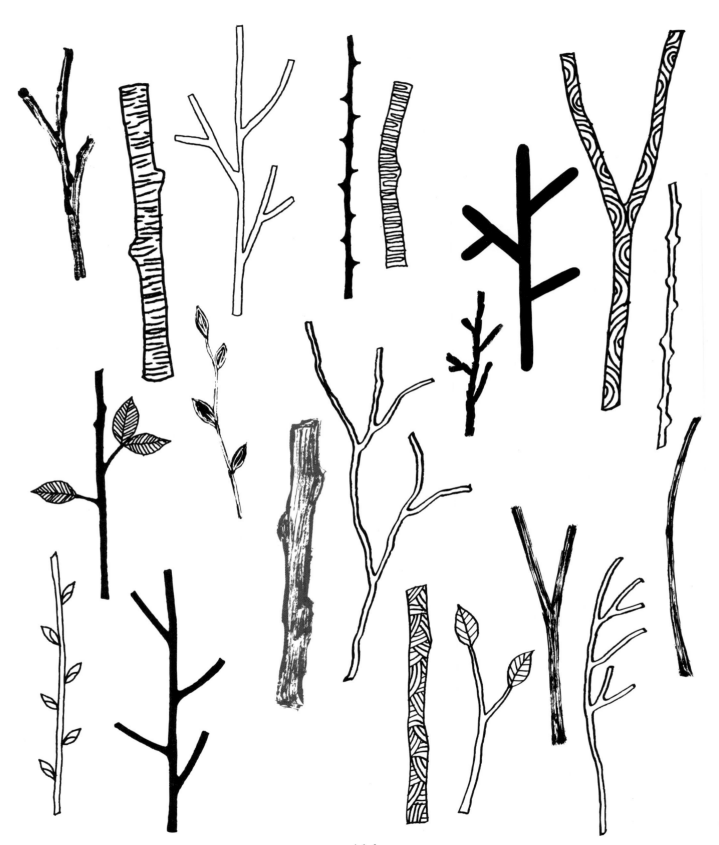

DRAW 20
TWIGS

DRAW 20
Dragonflies

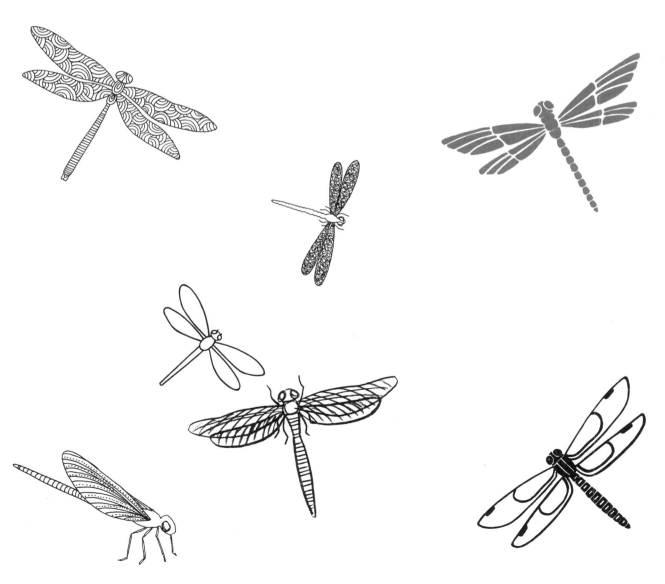

DRAW 20
Tulips

DRAW 20
GRAINS

DRAW 20
BEES

DRAW 20
seed heads

DRAW 20
MOTHS

DRAW 20
PEACOCK FEATHERS

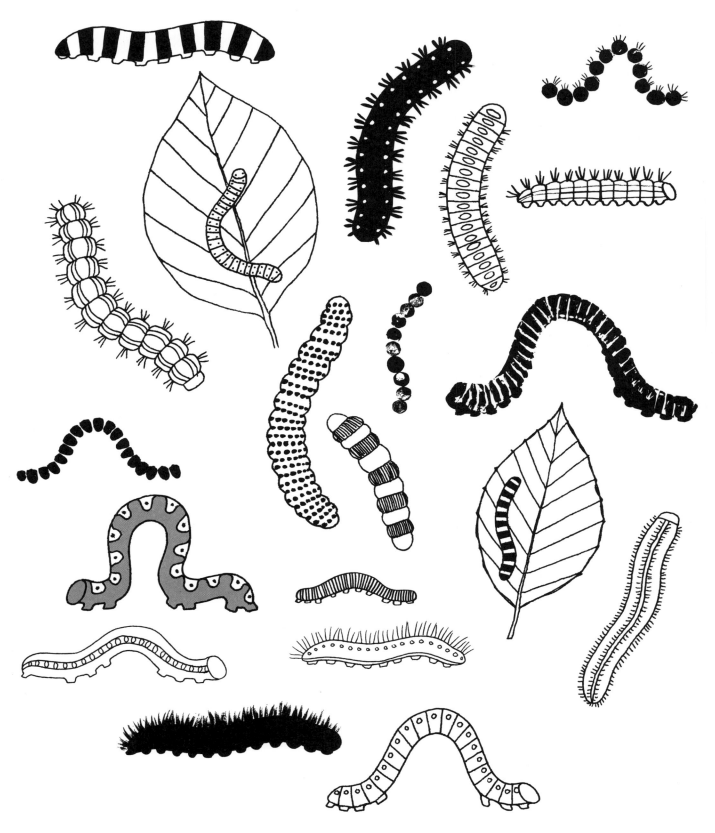

DRAW 20
caterpillars

DRAW 20
DANDELIONS

DRAW 20
DANDELIONS

DRAW 20
thistles

DRAW 20
butterflies

DRAW 20
root vegetables

DRAW 20
citrus fruits

SECTION 3
FLOWERS

Illustrations by Lisa Congdon

DRAW 20
Tulips

DRAW 20
DAFFODILS

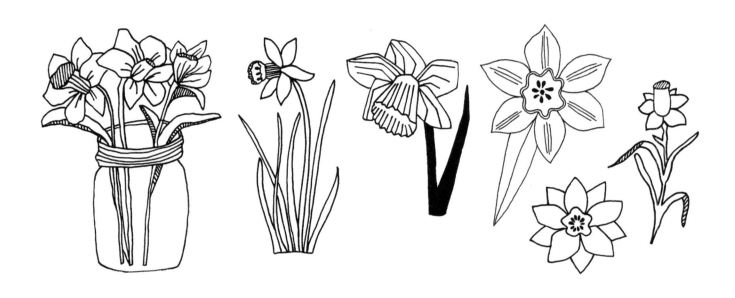

Ginger Blossoms

DRAW 20
Dahlias

DRAW 20

Roses

DRAW 20
DAISIES

DRAW 20
Lavender Plants

DRAW 20
Orchids

DRAW 20
Pansies

DRAW 20
Chrysanthemums

DRAW 20

Irises

DRAW 20

Marigolds

DRAW 20
Hollyhocks

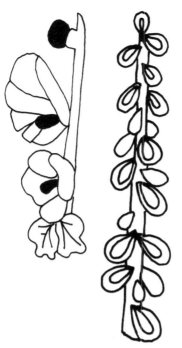

DRAW 20

Poppies

DRAW 20
Sunflowers

DRAW 20
PITCHER PLANTS

DRAW 20
Cherry Blossoms

Lotus Flowers

DRAW 20
Heather

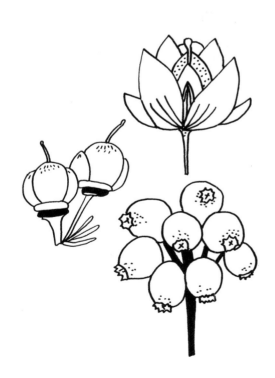

DRAW 20
maypops

DRAW 20
Honeysuckle

DRAW 20
CACTUS FLOWERS

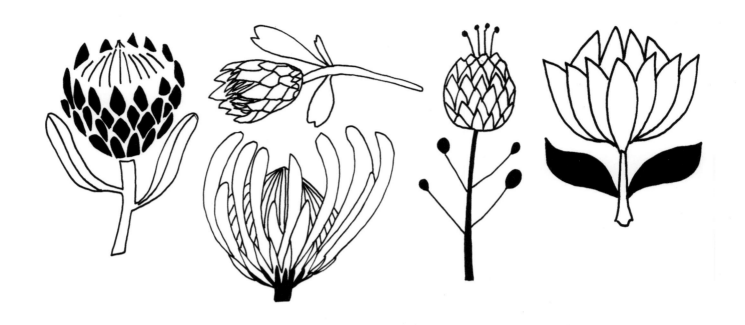

DRAW 20
Protea

DRAW 20
Geraniums

DRAW 20
Morning Glories

DRAW 20
Clovers

DRAW 20
Lilies

DRAW 20
Horse Nettle

DRAW 20
Bleeding Hearts

DRAW 20
Indian Blankets

DRAW 20
ASTERS

DRAW 20
Gladiolus

DRAW 20
Thistle

DRAW 20
Cone Flowers

DRAW 20
Bluebells

DRAW 20
Strawberry Plants

DRAW 20
Dandelions

DRAW 20
WAX PLANTS

DRAW 20
Foxgloves

Pomegranate Flowers

DRAW 20
BILLY BUTTONS

DRAW 20
Frangipani

DRAW 20
Birds of Paradise

DRAW 20
RANUNCULUS

DRAW 20
FREESIA

ABOUT THE ARTISTS

Fine artist and illustrator **Lisa Congdon** is best known for her colorful and detailed paintings and drawings. She enjoys hand lettering and pattern design, and keeps a popular daily blog about her work and life called "Today is Going to be Awesome." Lisa's clients include Quarry Books, Chronicle Books, Simon & Schuster, and the Museum of Modern Art, among others. She lives and works in Oakland, California. To see more of her work, visit Lisa's website at **www.lisacongdon.com**.

Julia Kuo grew up in Los Angeles and studied illustration and marketing at Washington University in St. Louis. She currently works as a freelance illustrator in Chicago. Julia designs stationery, illustrates children's books, concert posters, and CD covers and paints in her free time. One of her gallery shows featured paintings of street fashion shots from Face Hunter. Julia's clients include American Greetings, the *New York Times*, Little, Brown and Company, Simon and Schuster, Capitol Records, and Universal Music Group. She is also part of The Nimbus Factory, a collective of two designers and two illustrators specializing in paper goods. Her illustrations have been honored in *American Illustration, CMYK* magazine, and *Creative Quarterly*. **juliakuo.com**

Eloise Renouf graduated with a degree in printed textile design from Manchester Metropolitan University, UK. She worked as a fashion print designer in studios in both London and New York before establishing her own stationery company in 2000. She now designs and sells her own range of limited-edition prints and fabric accessories, whilst also undertaking commission and licensing work for homewares, stationery, and illustration. She lives and works in Nottingham, England, with her partner and three children. **www.eloiserenouf.etsy.com**

ALSO AVAILABLE

The Illustrated Emily Dickinson
Nature Sketchbook
978-1-63159-123-5

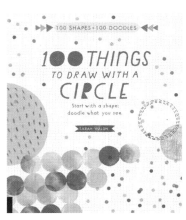

100 Things to Draw with a Circle
978-1-63159-137-2

100 Things to Draw with a Triangle
978-1-63159-100-6

The Paintbrush Playbook
978-1-63159-046-7

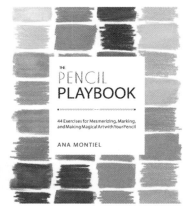

The Pencil Playbook
978-1-63159-058-0

The Marker Playbook
978-1-63159-125-9

The Pen & Ink Playbook
978-1-63159-124-2

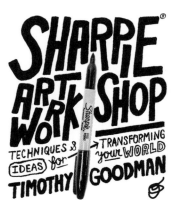

Sharpie Art Workshop
978-1-63159-048-1

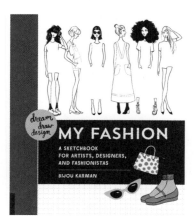

Dream, Draw, Design My Fashion
978-1-63159-097-9